West Chicago Public Library District
118 West Washington
West Chicago, IL 60185-2803
Phone # (630) 231-1552
Fax # (630) 231-1709

MONEDAS Y BILLETES
COINS AND MONEY

CINCO CENTAVOS
NICKELS

ELIZABETH MORGAN
TRADUCIDO POR ANA MARÍA GARCÍA

PowerKiDS
press

New York

Published in 2016 by The Rosen Publishing Group, Inc.
29 East 21st Street, New York, NY 10010

First Edition

Editor: Katie Kawa
Book Design: Katelyn Heinle
Spanish Translator: Ana María García

Photo Credits: Cover, p. 1 (piggy bank) Lizzie Roberts/Ikon Images/Getty Images; cover, pp. 6, 9, 10, 13, 14, 17, 18, 21, 24 (background design element) Paisit Teeraphatsakool/Shutterstock.com; cover, pp. 1, 5, 6, 9, 10, 13, 14, 17, 18, 22 (coins) Courtesy of U.S. Mint; pp. 5, 6, 9, 10, 13, 14, 18, 22 (vector bubbles) Dragan85/Shutterstock.com; p. 5 (girl) DAJ/Getty Images; p. 17 (Thomas Jefferson) John Parrot/Stocktrek Images/Getty Images; pp. 18, 24 (Monticello) Bob Stefko/The Image Bank/Getty Images; pp. 18, 21 (vector bubble) LAN02/Shutterstock.com; pp. 21, 24 (Buffalo nickel) Gregory James Van Raalte/Shutterstock.com; pp. 22, 24 (piggy bank) Ljupco Smokovski/Shutterstock.com.

Library of Congress Cataloging-in-Publication Data

Morgan, Elizabeth.
Nickels! = Cinco centavos / by Elizabeth Morgan.
p. cm. — (Coins and money = Monedas y billetes)
Parallel title: Monedas y billetes
In English and Spanish
Includes index.
ISBN 978-1-4994-0689-4 (library binding)
1. Nickel (Coin) — Juvenile literature. I. Morgan, Elizabeth. II. Title.
CJ1836.M674 2016
737.4973—d23

Manufactured in the United States of America

CPSIA Compliance Information: Batch #WS15PK: For Further Information contact Rosen Publishing, New York, New York at 1-800-237-9932

CONTENIDO

- -

CONTENTS

Podemos comprar cosas con monedas. Un *nickel* es un tipo de moneda.

We can buy things with coins. A nickel is one kind of coin.

DIEZ CENTAVOS
DIME

UN CENTAVO
PENNY

CINCO CENTAVOS
NICKEL

VEINTICINCO CENTAVOS
QUARTER

MEDIO DÓLAR
HALF-DOLLAR

Las monedas son dinero
hecho de metal.

Coins are money made of metal.

Un *nickel* es igual a cinco centavos.

One nickel is the same as five cents.

Un *nickel* es igual a
cinco *pennies*.

One nickel is the same as
five pennies.

Dos *nickels* son 10 centavos.
Esto es igual a un *dime*.

Two nickels are 10 cents.
This is the same as one dime.

13

Cinco *nickels* son igual a un *quarter*. ¿Cuántos centavos son?

Five nickels are the same as one quarter. How many cents is that?

Thomas Jefferson está en la parte delantera del *nickel*. Fue el tercer presidente de Estados Unidos.

Thomas Jefferson is on the front of the nickel. He was the third president of the United States.

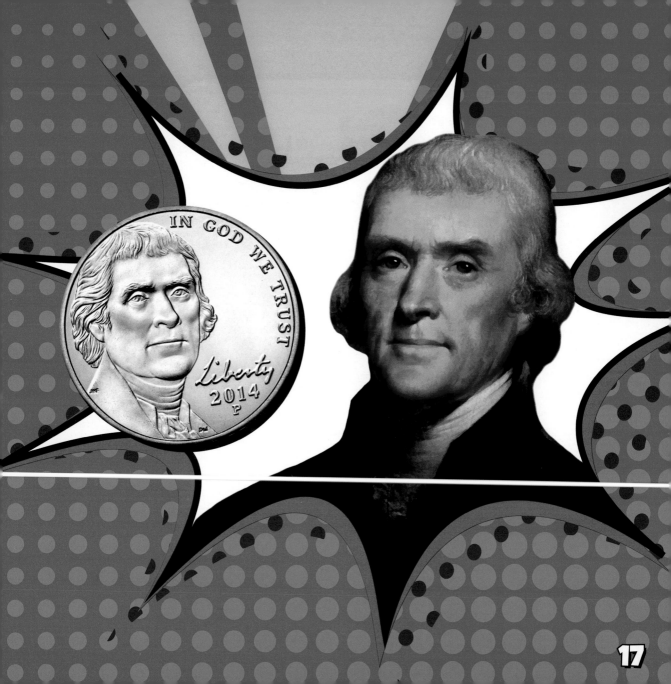

El edificio en la parte de atrás del *nickel* es la casa de Thomas Jefferson. Se llama **Monticello**.

The building on the back of the nickel is Thomas Jefferson's home. It is called **Monticello**.

El antiguo *nickel* tenía
un **búfalo**. Se conocía
como el *nickel* búfalo.

An old kind of nickel had
a **buffalo** on it. It was called
the Buffalo nickel.

Jordan tiene ocho *nickels* en su **alcancía**. ¿Cuántos centavos tiene?

Jordan has eight nickels in his **piggy bank**. How many cents does he have?

PALABRAS QUE DEBES APRENDER
WORDS TO KNOW

(el) búfalo
buffalo

Monticello
Monticello

(la) alcancía
piggy bank

ÍNDICE / INDEX

SITIOS DE INTERNET / WEBSITES

Due to the changing nature of Internet links, PowerKids Press has developed an online list of websites related to the subject of this book. This site is updated regularly. Please use this link to access the list: www.powerkidslinks.com/cam/nick